HOW TO SHOOT

HOW TO SHOOT

SOME LESSONS IN THE SCIENCE OF
SHOT GUN SHOOTING

By

ROBERT CHURCHILL

Introduction by Michael Brander

· THE ·
SPORTSMAN'S
PRESS
LONDON

Published by
The Sportman's Press, 1988

British Library Cataloguing in Publication Data

Churchill, Robert, *1886–1958*
How to shoot.
1. Sports : Shooting – Manuals
I. Title
799.2'13

ISBN 0–948253–31–2

Printed and bound in Great Britain by
Redwood Burn Limited, Trowbridge, Wiltshire

CONTENTS

Introduction

CONTENTS

CONTENTS

CONTENTS

Introduction By Michael Brander

THE NOVICE who is looking for a book on all aspects of how to shoot will find it in these pages. To a gunmaker's expertise Robert Churchill added the eye of the born teacher analysing every mistake with an unerring instinct. From his own immense experience of other people's faults and failings as well as his knowledge of guns and gunmaking he has successfully provided answers for all the most common errors.

Here he gets right down to the point and expounds his basic views on shooting, which are well worth following with care. The later, much enlarged edition, representing his views on game shooting, differed very little from many other books with the same or similar titles. It was certainly much longer, but in practice said very little more than this shorter book, in which his views are encapsulated without any frills.

Not even his most extreme critics, and there always have been critics of Churchill's views on XXV inch barrelled guns, would deny that he was an expert teacher in the shooting school and that his experience as the leading instructor of his day was second to none. I have personally always belonged to the school of thought holding to the principle that a gun should fit rather like a walking stick, or a comfortable suit. Too long a walking stick or an outsize suit on a short man can be as odd in appearance as too short a walking stick or jacket and trousers on a tall man. Churchill himself would probably have been the first to agree with this and, whether one accepts his views on barrel length or not, it must be admitted that in the shooting school he was absolutely first rate. In that respect alone this little book is undoubtedly well worth reprinting.

In stressing the need for constant practice, if only by handling the gun each day for a short session, he makes the all-important point that so many people forget when they put their gun away at the end of the season. For Robert Churchill the shooting season never ended; he was never without pupils in his shooting school. The importance of keeping in constant practice, like the keen golfer or efficient performer in any sport, has to be the secret of success and Churchill makes this point most effectively.

In many ways he was far in advance of his day. He was, for instance, the first to appreciate the importance of being able to demonstrate the pupil's faults to him and his use of the cine camera foreshadowed the more modern use of the video camera. By demonstrating to the pupil where he was making mistakes he was able to correct them, for once the error had been seen and understood it was more than half way to being overcome.

Not only was Churchill excellent at teaching people to shoot game, he was also amongst the first to appreciate the psychological approach in clay shooting. His comments on competition psychology are invaluable for anyone entering any form of clay competition from skeet to down-the-line. The importance of concentration on each individual shot is something that cannot be overstressed. As he emphasised this is something that applies equally to game shooting and to shooting clays. To treat each fresh shot as an individual challenge regardless of all else is the secret of good shooting. The same thing applies in, for instance, golf.

Correct gun mounting and stance, along with the importance of footwork and free swing are vitally important attributes of shooting and are covered, as might be expected, succinctly and well, along with the mysteries of correct alignment with the bird. It is in correction of all the common faults such as head movement and incorrect hand grip that he excels. In addition the question of eyesight and that surprisingly widespread weakness, a left master eye, are very adequately treated. Churchill's method of calculating forward allowance, another of the commoner old chestnuts, is also dealt with effectively.

Inevitably a gunmaker of his distinction has some sound remarks on the advantages or otherwise of the various types of stock and their effects on shooting. He also has some pointed comments to make on those people, and there are many of them, who fail to pay attention to the care of their guns, especially those lunatic enough to try to shoot out dents in their barrels apparently without appreciating that they are unwittingly weakening them to the stage where they may well be unsafe. He also makes the point as would any gunsmith of repute that a good gun is a worthwhile investment. If he could possibly have conceived in his wildest imagination the amazing prices a pair of his prewar best guns are making in today's market his remarks would have been in gilt edged type.

His chapter entitled 'Hints for Beginners' has some excellent points to make which cannot be too strongly emphasised. The photographs which accompany it illustrating various aspects of gun safety are delightful period gems as well as making their point well. I can strongly recommend this little book to any shooting man today. The comments the author makes are as sound now as they were when he first wrote them; any novice will benefit greatly from them and most experienced shooting men too. It deserves a place on every keen shooting man's bookshelf and should be taken out and re-read at intervals.

I

THE PERSONAL FACTOR

IN the five years since this book first appeared I have received a mass of correspondence—and I am extremely grateful to the sportsmen who sent it, since their letters were far better guidance than the kindliest or the bitterest of reviews.

The bulk of the criticism which I have received is perfectly sound. Some suggest that I should extend and elaborate the work. With this I do not agree—my reason being that I do not want to stress the " don't " side of the question. There are so many things to " do " that if you fill the mind of an anxious novice with a string of " don'ts," he is far too slow about his " do's." This may be a loose statement in written English, but it is at least sound psychology. I believe that a real advantage results from the adoption of the positive suggestion and that too great an insistence on the " don't " or negative side only enhances what psycholo-

gists would call the "inferiority complex"
of the unskilled shot. Elaboration or discussion is likely to send the mind off on a
train of thought for which in wing shooting
there is no time. Shot gun shooting is as
dependent as sound musketry on raw unargu-
able fact, and there is no room for discussion
or elaboration about the drill book which
produces marksmen out of recruits. Take my
instructions as drill, accept them, practise
them, and, above all, master them, not only
in abstract theory but in actual practice.

MUSCLE MEMORY

You may find this book easy to read, but
reading alone will not make you shoot. The
mind may accept the principle, but you have
also to build *muscle memory*. Your mind may
accept the new knowledge, but only practice
with the lesson in mind will ram it for ever into
your sub-consciousness. Concentrate on the
ideas and practise the technique—and, like
swimming, you will never forget it. When a
child masters the difficult feat of walking he
forgets how to walk—he knows how—but is
unaware of his knowledge as it is forgotten by
his conscious mind—he does it without
thinking. If anyone starts thinking about
walking such as when crossing a narrow plank

over a stream he does it unnaturally and
without confidence and is apt to falter. Again
consider the man learning to swim—until the
motions become a habit to him—until he ceases
to think of them, he is awkward—when he
is expert he does it without thinking. In
other words he has forgotten how to swim.
All this is to assure you that if you will
practise in your own room the motions
recommended in later pages you will gain
muscle memory and be able to mount your
gun properly without thought or effort.
Get a friend to act as company-sergeant-
major for you. Accept my statements as
you accept any formal drill, practise them
as a purely physical technique—without
argument—and then you will find that your
shooting has emerged from the mist of hazard
to a fairly steady average basis upon which
you can build your own individual style.

Style—there is no fixed standard; for
when all is said and done the personal
equation is paramount in shooting. A long-
armed, narrow-chested, tall man will inevitably have a different style as compared with
a short, broad-chested, short-armed man, but
when you come to analyse their performance,
there is very little, except the purely physical
difference, to influence the mechanics of the

process. The methods I advocate suit all physical variations, are easily learnt, and once learnt never forgotten. A secondary but no less important characteristic intervenes —*temperament*. This is a more disconcerting quality, for you will meet the quick, impatient type and the low velocity, enduring, patient slogger. The 'first is the hardest problem, for he is always in antagonism to himself. His mind outreaches his physical performance, and he is likely to swing to the other extreme, becoming casual, half-hearted and disappointed. Here discipline counts ; practice and success will cure that man. His biggest enemy is his own despondency, his quick reaction to failure. But if a mercurial spirit like this, once sees that he is getting better there is no more adept pupil and the mastery once gained lasts.

Your low velocity, patient slogger, presents another condition, but in a sense his shortcomings are his virtues. Slow to put into practice what he learns, yet once there it remains for ever. Nothing will shake it. He will always be a sound, clean shot.

There is no fixed style ; every man must develop his own style, but the basis of shooting is always and invariably dependent on the routine which I outline in this little book.

The eye alone cannot always adequately analyse either faults or the real ingredients of perfection. *The cine-camera* or the slow-motion camera, on the other hand, can render the greatest possible service for analysis. Here we have a point-by-point examination of the individual mechanism. I have already adopted the cine-camera as a mechanical adjunct for the determination of faults. It is invaluable for showing the sportsman his idiosyncrasies—a gun may fit perfectly, but a momentary hesitation or an error in mounting may negative the result of the best fitting gun which ever left a London workshop. Yet if you know where your own fault lies, you are three-quarters on the way to curing it. The film shows precisely where the error lies, and once known correction is easy.

II

GENERAL PRINCIPLES

NOT until one makes a critical survey of the wealth of books on shooting and sporting subjects which have appeared does one realise how few of them contain any practical matter on how to shoot with a shot gun.

We have in the English language what is probably the finest output of technical and sporting literature that can be found, yet if we contrast the treatment of shooting instruction with the detailed analysis that has been accorded to style in other games we become conscious of a great gap.

This is in essence due to the radical differences which exist between games which can be witnessed by a large audience and the comparative seclusion in which shooting is practised.

The average sportsman who shoots is seldom able to criticise or rather analyse the performance of his brother guns in the field. He is too busy, and his attention must necessarily be concentrated on his own sector

of the beat or drive.   His own style is in nine
cases out of ten a standard of unconscious
proficiency, the joint product of a well-fitting
gun, a good eye and past experience.   Ques-
tioned by an eager novice he can find few
golden rules to explain " how to shoot," and
in most cases candidly admits that it is more
a matter of " knack " or the personal equation
rather than any conscious formula or system
of technique.

The gunmaker who is a practical shot
himself and who is accustomed to studying
the actual shooting performance of his clients
approaches the problem from a different
standpoint.   He has had years of experience,
not only as a shot himself, but as a critic and
analyst of individual styles. His work of
fitting guns to clients gives him particular
opportunities of study, not limited to casual
glances at field performance during the shooting season, but a routine throughout the year.
In a sense he approximates to the coach,
amateur or professional, whose value and
authority are admitted in every other branch
of sport from lawn tennis to motor racing.
The gunmaker who does not shoot misses a
great opportunity.   Imagination is a poor
substitute for going through the mill.

The art of shooting is one that is just as

capable of being taught or learnt from fundamental points of style and technique as golf or tennis. In such games the attention paid to matters of grip, position and stance is rightly recognised as the highway to proficiency, and forms the basis of training which with practice develops into satisfactory achievement and good style. My method is to deal with the use of the game gun and the attainment of shooting skill on these modernised lines. Expert rifle and pistol shots have long since insisted on correct physical technique as the basis of all teaching in their particular branches of shooting. Careful study of shot gun shooting over many years has taught me that *certain fundamental rules which can be defined, are at the bottom of all good shot gun work and that disregard of these rules accounts for nearly all the bad shooting attributed to bad luck or other impersonal causes.*

THE SECRET OF GOOD SHOOTING IS SOUND FUNDAMENTAL TECHNIQUE IN STANCE, IN HANDLING THE GUN, IN MOUNTING IT TO THE SHOULDER AND IN AIMING.

Good shooting is an indefinite term at

best, for we all have varying standards by which we gauge our own and other folks' performance. We all know bad shots, poor shots, ordinary shots, fair shots, good shots, brilliant shots, and those happy beings, known as born shots. But these are all purely comparative terms. I would, for instance, make a difference between " good " and " brilliant " shots. A " brilliant " shot is a man whose standard of accuracy is as high as that of the " good " shot, but where the latter is cautious and does not fire at difficult birds, the " brilliant " man takes chances and as a result shows a lower percentage of kills to cartridges expended. On the other hand he probably kills more game in the day than the " good " shot, who is content only to take birds at easy angles—and of course he gets a good deal more fun out of it.

The " born " shot is the rare man who enjoys the consistent accuracy of the " good " shot in combination with the less calculated style of the " brilliant " shot. The success of the born shot is, however, due to the fact that consciously (or far more probably entirely unconsciously) he automatically obeys the underlying rules of the art and achieves perfect co-ordination of muscular movement and aim.

The average shot having read as far as
this has a very important question to ask :
" Can a middle-aged man alter the bad habits
he has already formed and develop into a
good shot ? "

Certainly he can, in fact he will improve
far more speedily than an absolute novice.
The absolute beginner is perhaps the most
difficult of all people to teach because he
" makes hard work of each shot." In a word
he uses far too much physical energy in his
movements and expends too much mental
calculation on his aim. He looks at the gun
rather than the bird, tries to improve his
first aim. He puts enough vigour into his
swing and " follow through " to lift a steam
engine, and lastly *stops* to pull the trigger—
thereby shooting behind his target.

Faults of style are easier to correct in men
who have done at least sufficient shooting
to have got over the preliminary troubles of
awkward muscular action with the gun,
who no longer flinch from fear of the noise or
recoil, and who have overcome the feeling
of strangeness inseparable from introduction
to any new sport. *Experience proves that
bad shooting habits can be eliminated at
almost any age and that an experienced shot
learns swiftly.*

The next problem is "Can a man teach himself to shoot?" He can, and a careful study of the detail in this book will help him enormously. But he cannot see his own faults as clearly as a bystander, and inevitably an expert coach can teach a man more in half a dozen lessons than he is likely to learn by himself in thrice the time.

If a man cannot find opportunity for a little work with a skilled coach he may do much by persuading a friend to go over with him the technique laid down in this book and then go out with him in the field. The friend, if he is an alert critic, will be able to indicate what appear to be the shooter's faults in the light of what he has just read.

Now let us proceed to the details of technique. For convenience sake these have been arranged in successive sections. They apply to right handed shots only. Left handed shots will appreciate that the details must be inverted or reversed to meet their personal equation.

III

STANCE AND FOOTWORK

You will often notice that experienced shots, standing in a ploughed field and waiting for a drive to commence, are at some pains to select a position where there is no obstacle to impede their stance and footwork. They tread down a ridge or select a wide furrow to secure a position for their feet which is both firm and free from obstructions such as would prevent their pivoting.

Above all the balance and poise of the body must be firm and comfortable whereby the weight is supported evenly on *both legs*. The only exception occurs when using wild-fowl guns or unusually heavy charges, in which cases the greater portion of the weight may be thrown on the left leg.

The feet should be some nine inches apart, a distance which will of course vary slightly with the general build of the individual.

Figure 1 shows the common fault of standing with *heels too close* together. The result is that the bulk of the recoil is taken by

" POINT YOUR BODY AT THE BIRD "

The forward inclination of the body with weight on left foot for ground game.

Weight back on the right foot for the overhead shot.

Any " free " position may be adopted whilst waiting for the drive to commence

Weight on the right foot : left heel turned for the bird crossing to the right.

Weight on the left foot with right heel uplifted and turned for the shot on the left.

See page 22

HOW TO GRIP THE STOCK.

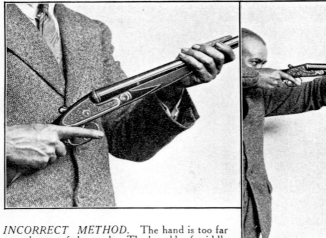

INCORRECT METHOD. The hand is too far over the top of the stock. The knuckle of middle finger is hard against the guard. The gun cannot be mounted without raising the elbow thus causing head movement. Finger and arm are likely to be bruised on recoil.

CORRECT METHOD. The hand is more under the stock thus straightening the trigger finger and clearing the knuckle. The gun can be mounted without raising the elbow and without head movement.

See page 28

HOW TO GRIP THE BARRELS.

A

B.

A. *INCORRECT METHOD.* The fingers encroach over the rib, causing the gun to " cant " or to mount high on an object.

B. *CORRECT METHOD.* The left thumb on top of the left barrel encourages pointing ; prevents up-jump ; prevents the finger tips covering the rib and allows the ball of the thumb to be made prominent thus blocking the sight of the gun from the sight of the left eye and ensuring right eye domination.

See page 30

THE READY POSITION.

A. Incorrect method: the muzzle "up in the air."

B. Can easily be dropped too low of the mark.

E. Correct method: keep the stock tight under the arm until the muzzle (left hand) is pointing at the bird.

C. Another incorrect method which causes shooting low of the mark.

D. The butt reaches the shoulder before the muzzle is on the bird (incorrect).

See page 34

the shoulder without assistance from the legs. This is not only unnecessarily wearying to the shooter, but also prevents him firing a successful second barrel until he has recovered his poise. In addition it is a frequent means of causing bruised cheek or second finger. Shots who may suffer from these troubles should suspect their stance and be at pains to correct it.

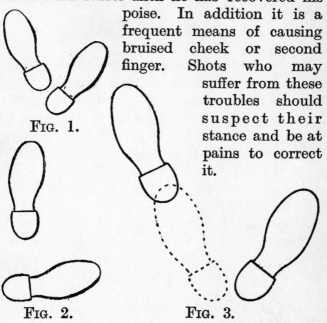

FIG. 1.

FIG. 2.   FIG. 3.

Figure 2. Another fault. *Right foot immediately behind left.*—This twists the body in such a manner that the gunstock is not firm to the shoulder. As a result the recoil on the discharge of the first barrel causes the butt to shift from the shoulder to the arm

muscle.   Thus the second barrel cannot
be fired with true alignment.   This fault is
perhaps the most frequent cause of second
barrel misses.   The butt must bed squarely
into the shoulder.

Figure 3.   *The Correct Position.*—Its effect
is to combine body and legs as a resilient
spring for taking up the recoil.   In addition
turning is easily and smartly accomplished.
To accustom yourself to take up this stance,
firstly stand comfortably with heels close
together, then take half a step forward with
the left foot ; this should bring you to the
correct stance.

Footwork.—Directly associated with the
correct stance is the capacity for proper
footwork.   They are interdependent.   With
a crossing shot coming from right to left
raise the right heel and pivot on the right
toe, keeping the left foot flat and firm to the
ground.   With a shot crossing from left to
right reverse the action.   Test this with a
gun in your hand in the privacy of your
room and determine for yourself the position
of feet and distance between them which
gives you the best poise and the widest
freedom of " follow through " or swing.
*You will find that three-quarters of the complete
circle is easily covered by this method.*

When birds are immediately behind, you may be able *on firm ground* to move one foot more to the rear of the other one, with its toe turned as much as is conveniently possible in the direction of the bird; then follow the directions in " Footwork " of raising the other heel and pivotting.

To get round on the right, shift the right foot a few inches to the rear of the left and the reverse for the opposite side. Do not take a step with the foot, since to lift it off the ground disturbs the balance, rather " scrape " it round to the back of the other one.

In partridge driving fast birds often get out of range before a gun can get round, and this movement should be practised in your room against your usual method, to enable you to decide whether you can adopt it for such shots. It is difficult at first, but after practice you will become more confident and be able to do this movement very smartly whilst retaining your balance. With a little indoor drill the motions become automatic.

This business of indoor drill is well worth while, for just as a boxer uses a punch ball for practice and exercise, so a shooter can improve his style and get into better muscular trim for field work by a little indoor snapping practice.

The preliminary manual of rifle exercise in the army is not solely to teach the recruit how to open and load his rifle. It is very largely designed to accustom him to the muscular exercise involved. If you give a man unaccustomed to guns a weapon to handle his movements are relatively slow and uncouth. He has to exert far more energy than the trained man.

We put our guns away at the end of January, and when August or September arrives, even if we have been accustomed to shooting all our lives, we are to a certain extent slack and out of this particular form of training. Many of the very best shots, men with established reputations as leading performers, go down to shooting grounds before the season opens and fire on two or three successive days in order to get into training. This practice braces them, accustoms them to recoil—and it must be remembered that the physical effort of lifting a six and a half pound gun and firing a hundred or so rounds is considerable : it puts them into physical training as well as " gets their eye in." Not every one can spare the time for these visits, but indoor drill, although it lacks the element of actual practice and the reality of recoil, is by no means waste of time—it is, nevertheless, sound physical training.

Those who live in the country, or pay frequent visits, can find many opportunities for carrying a gun and firing a sufficient number of rounds to maintain what I might term " contact " with their gun. In the spring sowing season a large number of cartridges are expended in crop protection; this is also the time when game-keepers get busy with winged vermin. Later on the half-grown rabbits come into season, whilst August marks the opening of duck shooting. Throughout the fruit season many promising crops are ruined. In a word, the keen shooting man enjoys sundry opportunities to combine valuable practice with protection of the country's food supplies.

IV

GRIP

Take your gun and go over this section carefully *with the weapon in hand*. Grip is a very important matter and it is necessary that the detail should be understood.

Right Hand.—Most people think that they grip a gun naturally and correctly. All too often they do not. The tendency is to carry the right hand far too much round the top of the stock. This checks it coming up and forces the knuckle of the second finger hard against the rear of the trigger guard (another cause of bruised finger).

Make this test: Lift your gun to your shoulder with your thumb purposely too far round the top of the stock. You will find that you cannot lift the gun without raising the elbow as well. That in itself causes muscular constraint and awkwardness.

And, again, starting with your usual grip, re-adjust *so that the finger tips of the right hand are rather more round the stock than usual.* You will find that the gun fits com-

fortably into the hollow of the hand and that
it can be lifted without any elbow work far
more quickly and comfortably than usual,
also you will be able to bring the gun up to
the cheek instead of having to put your cheek
down ready to meet the gun.

A frequent cause of bad grip is the tendency
for shooters with a short thumb to keep it
in contact with the top lever. This is not
necessary, as the fraction of time lost in
shifting the grip of the hand is immaterial,
whereas a bad grip means bad shooting.

The strength or pressure with which the
stock is held should not be exaggerated.
The gun should be brought up with a fairly
light grip which should be tightened *only* at
the instant of trigger pressure. If you grip
too tightly while mounting the gun to the
shoulder you may relax on the instant of
firing. Bruised cheek or finger is sometimes
an indication of too light a right hand grip
at the instant of firing, though more usually
due to the error in stance indicated in the
previous section.

Sometimes a man may use a gun which he
has inherited or bought second-hand. It
may fit, but very much more likely it does not.
Stock length, bend and cast-off represent
only approximations to fit unless we also take

c

into account the circumference of the narrow
portion of the stock where the right hand
grips it. Men's hands vary considerably.
One may have a long-fingered, trim and
flexible hand, another a broad-palmed, capable
hand, that of a surgeon rather than an artist,
while a third may have a short-fingered,
podgy hand. Even if all these three are
relatively the same in the circumference
which they can grip, the width of the hand
varies. When fitting a gun I pay considerable
attention to this factor. One man may need
the comb of his stock cutting back half or
three-quarters of an inch more toward the
heel than another—simply in order to make a
comfortable bedding for his hand. There is
no particular novelty about this attention to
manual anatomy, for in the old days when
duelling was in vogue a gentleman would be
measured for his pistols, the selection of an
appropriately shaped stock having been part
and parcel of the gunsmith's craft. They had
to fit perfectly in the individual hand.
Similarly in these modern days we must
ensure that our game guns are stocked to fit
not only the bodily dimensions of clients,
but also fit their hands.

In my opinion the grip of every normal gun
should be tapered from the direction of the

breech, that is to say, it should be thicker in front of the hand than at the rear, and thus offer a cone to prevent the hand slipping forward on recoil.

Very often one sees a grip tapered the reverse way. Such guns tend to slip through the fingers on recoil with bruised second finger for result.

Left Hand Grip.—The right and left hands should each do an equal share of the work of lifting the gun to the shoulder. The correct point of reach is found by balancing the gun between the two hands until the point of equal distribution of weight is found.

If the left hand is too far back the stock will mount earlier than the barrels, which will " sag," also the recoil will be more heavily felt on the shoulder.

If the left hand is too far forward the barrels come up before the stock. This is almost as bad.

The gun should be balanced to encourage horizontal lifting, so that by the time the butt touches the shoulder the barrels should be pretty well parallel to the line set by the eyes.

A badly balanced gun has no right place for the front grip, but one properly balanced will allow firm grasp to be taken near the front of the fore-end.

The left thumb should not be curled round the barrel but rather be held lengthwise and made to project, or at least be noticeable. This serves a double purpose, for it cuts out disturbance of aim due to left eye vision and also prevents the fingers covering too much of the barrel and encroaching on the sighting rib and also prevents the barrels jumping out of hand on recoil—another cause of bruised cheek.

While lifting the gun the barrels should only be held lightly—but they should be gripped at the instant of firing.

V

THE first and most important convention of the shooting field prescribes that in no circumstance shall a gun, loaded or unloaded, point towards anyone. The unpleasant yet necessarily important task of the host is to warn a man who cannot manage his gun safely and, should a further breach occur, to ask him to leave the field. *In theory a gun is always loaded.* A man who from lack of control, abnormal excitability or inadequate training is careless in his handling of a gun should be disciplined at once. Permanent physical injury to an individual at the hands of a careless gun handler is a serious affair, while any temporary embarrassment due to the affronted pride of somebody being called to order, is at worst a transient matter in comparison.

There are two safe positions in which sporting guns are customarily carried when shooting is not afoot : (1) on the shoulder with the muzzles pointing skyward—*not horizon-*

tally inclined ; (2) in the crook of the elbow with the muzzles pointing downward. The latter is probably the favourite method of carrying a gun, and, though theoretically slightly less safe than the shoulder position, it is as good in practice.

When walking up game or at the stand waiting for birds the gun is held by both hands in easy position. A double injunction is here necessary : keep it pointing forward and as motionless as possible.

From the safe carrying, walking or waiting position the sportsman comes to the " ready." This is not the same as the kindred military position, for with a shot gun the " ready " position is one in which the stock is about twelve inches below the shoulder, the butt forward of the arm or only slightly tucked in and the barrels horizontal and *not* inclined at 30° as is the military fashion.

Thus held the gun is rightly poised to come on to a straight away bird with the minimum of delay, and in the case of birds at an angle the turn of the body carries the arms with it *and so achieves correct alignment without motion of the arms themselves.*

VI

GUN MOUNTING

THIS is perhaps the most critical process of shooting, for it co-ordinates all the mechanical functions of stance, footwork and grip with the conscious function of aim.

When you point your finger at an object you aim at it and there is unconscious adjustment of the line of vision with the axial line of the pointing finger. Point at an object, glance along your extended finger and note how you have without conscious sighting taken a true aim.

The left or forward hand must be not considered simply as a lifting lever for the gun. You must, so to speak, mentally aim or point at the object with the left hand which holds the gun. You point just as straight with your left forefinger as you do with your right. Drive the left hand forward with a vigorous pointing movement—pointing at the bird the whole time.

The left hand does the real aiming. But the right must keep pace with the left, doing its share of directing the muzzle on the object the whole time that the gun is coming up.

Here is where gunfitting and to less extent the clothes worn need consideration. The gun must not be too long in the stock or the clothes bulkier or tighter than those normally worn while shooting. On the other hand though the stock should barely scrape the coat neither may it be too short. In practice half-an-inch is a fair clearance and the forward thrust of the left arm automatically provides it.

At the completion of the mounting movement or rather this first portion of it, the gun is up to the eye-level and the butt of the stock *in touch with but not home* on the shoulder. The left hand will be pointing at the object in subconscious co-ordination with the sight or line of vision from the eye. Now, *with the right hand only* pull the stock smartly back and in to the shoulder and at the same time contract the trigger finger *so that as the gun is snapped back to the shoulder by the right hand the trigger is pulled exactly at the limit of this backward movement. Swing is combined with this movement.*

It is in appearance almost a " snap " and the jar of the stock against the shoulder aids the trigger finger in precise timing of its pull. Analysing this simple yet complex movement we find that the left arm pushes forward while the right neutralises the push and adds the bit extra that brings the gun back. Thus the left arm absorbs a large proportion of the recoil which would otherwise be received on the shoulder.

The pulling of the stock back to the shoulder by the right hand involves the necessary grip by this hand and so avoids the occasional trouble of bruised middle finger from too slack a grip. With practice the opposing movement of the two arms becomes so automatic that the trigger finger can be left semi-rigid and the actual firing by trigger pressure can be made (indeed should be made) part and parcel of the butting of the gun to the shoulder. Trigger pulling thus takes its time from the butt reaching the limit of its travel to the shoulder.

From the foregoing you will see that the *eyes have been left nothing to do but look at the bird*. The hands and arms automatically obey the eyes, and *if the gun is mounted correctly—discharge occurs automatically and in perfect time as the butt comes to the shoulder.*

Provided the gun fits and that the quarry is within range you will shoot exactly where you are looking and should kill every time.

Obviously every bird killed is proof that

the muzzle must have been pointed in the right place—next, that as the barrels lie in the left hand this also was pointing in the right place. Combining the two propositions one shoots wherever the left hand points. If weakness or injury prevents or makes this ordinary procedure at all difficult there are remedies dealt with in another chapter.

When this formula is properly carried out misses occur from one cause—and one cause only—*not looking at the proper place.* Curiously enough when you have mastered the knack of correct gun mounting, misses which before you could not analyse or diagnose but attributed vaguely to some fanciful cause are easily resolved. *You know instinctively what you have done wrong and are able to correct the error.* The only explanation I can offer is that the shooter knows where he is putting his charge because the slightly upward movement of recoil lifts the muzzle of the gun into view and the eye takes cognisance.

A common complaint of shooters is that they " do no good with their second barrel." This is often attributed to disturbance of the grip or shoulder bedding of the gun by the recoil of the first discharge. The method of gun mounting I indicate above eliminates this. If the left arm is correctly pushed forward it not only serves to keep the butt from scrubbing against the clothes (so that an extra heavy coat in hard weather does not so seriously disturb or upset the fit of your gun), but, acting as a girder under compression against the backward pull of the right hand, it takes the main stress of recoil and absorbs it without transmitted shock to the body. A bad mounter, on the other hand, takes the full recoil shock on his shoulder instead of on his left arm and *in consequence is swung slightly round, so that for his second shot he has perforce to establish his aim again.* Hence misses with the second barrel.

The foregoing remarks deal with the " going away " bird, perhaps the simplest shot of all, but the subsequent instruction detailing the adaptation of the technique to more difficult shots are all dependent on this first mastery of the knack of correct gun mounting.

A novice is inclined to snatch the gun to his shoulder. This is wrong. The whole sequence of movement for ordinary shots should be easy and steady, becoming in time so purely mechanical that once learnt is never forgotten.

Contrast this technique with the practice so often seen of raising the gun at an angle rather than parallel to the line of vision, then bringing the muzzle down on the bird. In this practice it is obvious that not only is the line of vision temporarily intercepted by the barrels, but that the gun is spinning windmill fashion, and it has to be got out of its spin before firing takes place. With proper technique *the muzzles are finding the bird during the whole time of mounting,* and even a slightly premature or a belated trigger pressure does not necessarily involve the miss that is unavoidable in the case of the man " tip-catting " his gun or otherwise not keeping his muzzles in the general direction of the bird.

In the field it is not possible to ensure a succession of pure " straight away " shots for practice purposes, but a good deal can be done with simple manual exercise in one's room at home. Practise gun mounting with a pair of " snap caps " in the barrels, and you will in a day or so get the necessary muscular control or " knack " which is half the battle.

Timing the discharge is rather more difficult at the start and can really only be learnt by practice, preferably at clay birds. In essence there should be a ratio between the speed of the bird and the speed of mounting the gun to the shoulder. *The swifter birds need a quicker movement.*

After a little practice this soon ceases to be a matter of conscious calculation, but just an automatic or reflex effect accomplished instinctively and without thought.

Those who are dogged by persistent failure are sure to ask the question, "Does my gun fit me ? " It is not one that can be answered in general terms, but if you do not shoot well and your gunfitter has not seen you shoot, it is highly probable that some alteration is needed. The modern gunfitter who treats his work as a profession and something more than a department of salesmanship realises that it is waste of time and the client's money to fit him with a gun having bend or cast-off designed to compensate for faults in his manner of gunmounting. These should be corrected not by deforming the gun but by instructing the client. Unless he has been properly trained or has unconsciously and naturally evolved a good consistent technique of his own, his very errors are inconstant and it is useless to try to attempt a fit until a standard or basis has been established.

Granting the ever-increasing number of good shots the average is still a low one, and there is much scope for improvement. An absolute beginner can after a few lessons be fitted with a gun which is really suitable for him. He will in most cases be above the average even after this short training. A man who is a practised but mediocre shot will improve under tuition from the beginning and can be properly trained in half the time required by an absolute novice.

A perfect fit with a gun is dependent on the establishment of a preliminary normal method or standard of shooting, with subsequent small alterations and adaptations to suit the maturing style. No gunmaker or fitter, however expert, can hope to make a gun a perfect fit for a client by forecasting what he will become when he has mastered the groundwork of gun handling.

The old-fashioned principle of trial and error by the gunmaker and trial by the client is now outworn, and it is desirable that the client should master basic requirements of good shooting, proper stance, grip and the technique of gun mounting before anything more than a broad outline of the ultimate gun is attempted. He will get far more pleasure out of his sport, and it is also far more satisfactory to the gunmaker, for it gives him a solid foundation to work on. If he knows his art as a gunfitter he can be certain of a completely satisfied client.

From the client's point of view he will

be doubly benefited, because gun-fitting so conducted includes shooting lessons of a kind to lay the foundations of future success.

The stress which has been laid on having a gun fit properly would not be complete without a companion warning not to be finnicky when once all the service that fitting can render has been performed. The man who seeks in the fit of his gun an explanation for every miss and condemns it outright when he is temporarily out of form is liable to get into an unsettled state that will postpone natural recovery. In extreme cases those who expect too much from gun fitting visit one professor after another, and as most have ideas and fancies a good case can be made out for changes, some of them involving a fresh purchase. Provided a gun is as near right as an experienced and conscientious expert can make it the shooter should abolish all doubt and concentrate on making himself master of the weapon. There is much for him to do, for instance break himself of any bad habits that a previous gun of poor fit has engendered. In general, he must perform the final act of fitting, that is fit himself to the gun and as soon as may be, give it the status of an old favourite.

VII

THE THEORY OF ALLOWANCE

THE man who has mastered the foregoing technique as applied to the straight-away shot will find that it equally applies to crossing and overhead shots so soon as the need for extra allowance in these cases has been appreciated.

The action of keeping the left hand pointing at the moving bird automatically compels a correct swing of the whole body and the gun comes to the shoulder without a check for aiming or trigger pressure—but all in one harmonious movement.

Contrast this with the style of the man who shoulders his gun and then chases the bird with the muzzle, making either a calculated or an empirical " allowance " forward of his target. His endeavour to compensate for speed may be justified in theory but bad trigger pulling results in practice.

The " allowance " principle, when permitted to enter into shooting as a distraction is quite unsuited to the average sportsman and,

if imperfectly understood, a prolific source of
irritation and error.   Take a simple demon-
stration of its difficulty.

A charge of shots takes 1/20th of a second
to travel 20 yards ; 1/10th, 30 yards ; 1/7th,
40 yards.   A bird travelling at 40 miles per
hour covers one, two and three yards respectively in the same time intervals 1/20, 1/10
and 1/7th of a second, and we know that the
gun must be pointed these distances ahead to
score or kill.

But measure out the ranges in straight line
in an open field or paddock and erect three
poles at 20, 30 and 40 yards respectively.
Now attach a piece of whitewashed board 1
yard in length as a crosspiece to the pole at
20 yards, a 2 yard one to the 30 yard pole
and a three yard one to the 40 yard pole.

Then return to the firing point and look
at them.   They will present a very neat
example of how easily the eye is deceived,
for in perspective they all look about the
same size and they all look far shorter than
they really are.   The inference to be drawn is
that a constant angular allowance suffices, to
be modified and made more precise as experience increases.

A short study of the illustration will con-
vince you how hopeless it is to attempt to

D

calculate precise allowances for varying ranges in the heat of shooting. Once you appreciate that allowance is needed, let eye and swing collaborate to procure the correct measure.

The whole secret is to regularise your movements and mount the gun properly to the shoulder so that the hand and eye co-ordinate. Your barrel must always be aligned precisely where your eye is looking. The eye learns its job quickly enough. Apparently you are shooting straight at the bird, but unconsciously you will be making all necessary allowances.

PRACTICE THE POINTING OF THE LEFT HAND AND BODY AT THE BIRD FROM THE "READY" POSITION UNTIL YOU ARE DOING IT INSTINCTIVELY WITHOUT BEING CONSCIOUS OF DOING IT.

VIII

OVERHEAD AND CROSSING SHOTS

THE difference between shooting at birds overhead and crossing, as compared with going-away, is that besides being in more rapid flight their line of travel is more or less at right angles with the line of fire and, therefore, the gun must be directed further ahead than with the going-away bird. What I propose to teach is that the more rapid gun movement caused by the body swing automatically carries the aim more forward. If you mount your gun at a speed that is equal to the speed of the bird ; or in other words, if you keep your left hand pointing at the bird during the whole of the gun mounting, then if it is a slow incomer the unconscious over-throw is very slight, but all that is needed for correct forward allowance. On the other hand if it is a very fast crossing shot your own speed is increased . . . the overthrow is proportionately greater and is again the correct forward allowance. . . . TRAIN THE EYE AND HAND TO TAKE CHARGE OF

THESE MATTERS AND LEARN THEIR JOB WITHOUT BRAIN INTERFERENCE.

Once again remember the remarks on stance and footwork in Section III.

If your technique is sound you will find the right angle target, whether overhead or wide out, presents no difficulties. Once again dismiss all idea of calculated allowances. Look at the bird, pivot easily and smoothly, and complete the movement as for a straight-away shot, *but without in any way checking your swing.*

If it seems difficult to begin with, then adopt a slow smooth body swing before mounting the gun. *Above all do not mount the gun and then swing*—this is hopeless.

Readers will note that in the foregoing sections they have never been told to look along their barrels or to keep their sight in view. *Don't.*

In practice the shooter should not be conscious of his gun muzzle, the rib or sight. *His eye, or rather his attention, should be fully occupied with the bird, and if he holds his gun properly he will hit whatever he is looking at.*

When the gun has been fired recoil jars the barrels up and the shooter may then see them, but with proper action and a well fitting gun he should not be conscious of them till he has fired.

The scientific basis for this is the fact that the eye cannot pay attention to objects at different ranges at one and the same time. In rifle shooting it is necessary to focus the target, and yet at the same time see the front sight. The backsight he trues up with the foresight first of all, and then deals with foresight and bull, usually by means of an intermediate focus. Shot gun practice is different. There is no time for focus to pass from one object to another. Gun fitting gets breech and sight into line with the eye. For the rest the close range and the wide-spread circle of pellets will compensate for any small inaccuracy of alignment or centreing.

At the moment of striking a billiard player looks at the object ball, not at the cue tip or his own ball. The golfer; after he has adjusted his stance and rehearsed his swing, has to keep his eye on the ball and not on his club. In Tennis, Cricket, and in fact all such sports, the eye must be kept on the object. *So the shooting man must keep his eye on the bird and ignore his gun.*

If your eye is focussed on your gun you will mount behind an incoming bird and will have great difficulty in catching up with it.

IX

POSITION OF THE HEAD

IT is not generally recognised that this rather important factor is closely associated with eyesight or vision. A boy will usually lower his head to meet the stock, but a middle-aged man will hold his head erect and raise the gun to his face.

These two characteristics cover the difference between " young sight " and " old sight," and nothing is commoner than a marked falling off in shooting due to an unsuspected change in eyesight in middle age.

A man may have been shooting all his life with a straight stocked gun. The change of vision occurs and he finds he is right off his shooting. The cure is not glasses, but a bending down of the gunstock about a quarter of an inch at the heel or bump. This will compensate for the alteration to alignment due to the new head position.

Whilst on this subject it is as well to mention that relaxation of the muscles from age or sedentary habits also alters gun fit, and a shorter stock will be found more comfortable with increasing age. Similarly a novice who has yet to learn how to extend his arms fully and naturally in the normal shooting position should begin with a gun rather short for him. When properly practised he can be fitted for exact length, a simple matter of fitting a different depth of heel-plate.

To test your own gun follow out the section on correct gun mounting, and note if, when you press the trigger, the rib and muzzle of the gun are correctly levelled " on " the object.

The best position for the head is fairly erect and turned very slightly to the right.

If you have to put your head too much down to the stock you are not properly fitted. Above all the head must be naturally, normally and comfortably poised. It is hopeless to try to adapt the poise of head and neck to a badly fitted gun, for it induces rapid fatigue and consequent falling off in shooting. A proper grip of the right hand will allow the stock to come up to the face. The head is inclined slightly to avoid the cheekbone or jawbone pressing hard on the stock, the cheek should touch midway between the two.

Head position is an arbitrary habitude which varies with the individual. It should be firstly and above all things " natural," fairly erect and definitely firm. Gun headache is due in nine cases out of ten to a neglect of one thing only, the neck muscles are not braced and the head is held " loose." The shock of recoil jerks the head and the effect is that of a minor " knock out " blow. The old remedy of holding a rubber band between the teeth is a sound one, for the act of clenching the teeth steadies the head and stiffens the neck muscles, so that the automatic throw-back of the head is lessened. Most shooters automatically retract their neck muscles and bring their head down to their shoulders when firing. A minority—and particularly the long-necked minority—do not do this, and complain of gun headache in consequence. Alter the attitude and alter the gun to fit is the real remedy for your headache. It is an entirely curable trouble.

Sometimes one finds people who believe that by adopting one particular load or one particular brand of powder they escape from headache, but you will find upon inquiry that they do not agree about the powder. One will claim that he is headache-free when he uses say 42 grains of Schultze, another

says that that is the worst possible load for
him, and that for his part he cannot use
other than 33-grain E.C. without a headache.
Recoil, the note of vibration of the explosion,
all are called in to account for the trouble,
but actually it comes from one and the same
cause—taking the recoil shock with a loosely
held head. Set the head down into the
shoulders, though without raising the
shoulders, stiffen the neck muscles, and gun
headache will vanish !

The position of the head and above all
the rigid maintenance of that position are
very vital matters in shooting. In golf it
is recognised that head movement while a
shot is being taken will seriously affect its
direction ; a lift of the head may cause you
to miss your ball, a slight inclination may
lead you to hit below it. Golfers know that
if they envisage the ball as a whole they are
prone to " top " it, whereas if they concentrate on the back, viz. a point on the ball,
greater precision is achieved.

The underlying principles apply in a similar
sense to head movements during gun mounting. A great many of those unaccountable
misses at seemingly easy " away birds " are
due to too much head movement during gun
mounting. One's vision is centred on the

bird, but as the gun is raised there is a risk of final unconscious squeeze of the face down to meet the stock—and a consequent loss of the instinctive accuracy of first aim.

Remember that if you lift your head you tend to shoot over your birds. If you lower the head you tend to shoot low.

Summarising the points you must remember that once the eye has found the object the head should be carried rigid, and not moved independently of the body. This requires practice and at first concentration, but once learnt becomes instinctive, and will often show both improvement in speed and in accuracy.

" *Keep your eye on the bird.*"   The eye must not leave the bird in order to look ahead and attempt to estimate a forward distance, a correct allowance. Shooters who do this usually leave their gun lagging imperceptibly behind, but if you look straight at the head of the bird you will unconsciously make all necessary allowance.

X

EYESIGHT AND THE MASTER EYE

Eyesight.—This is a matter for oculists, but within limits poor eyesight is no bar to good shooting.

Shot gun shooting takes place at such short ranges that faults of vision which debar a man from accurate rifle shooting do not seriously affect shot gun practice.

If a man can recognise the difference between a pheasant and a partridge in rapid flight at forty yards he will be able to shoot with ordinary efficiency.

The Master Eye.—A good deal has been talked and written about this particular problem and the simplest outstanding fact has been overlooked.

In the normal man the degree of " master eyedness " is slight. What is not so well-known is that fatigue of the master eye rapidly transfers the mastery (temporarily of course) *from one eye to the other.*

If you strain and weaken the command of your right eye by putting your head down to the stock of a badly fitting gun or by a bad habit of gun mounting you tire the eye. *After a few such shots the right eye is fatigued and the left then takes mastery.*

This phenomenon is recognised by rifle shots who close or half close the left eye in order to prevent the disturbance of vision consequent on fatigue of the right or aiming eye. Yet it has not, so far as I am aware, ever been noted as an important factor in shot gun shooting.

In other sports this eye problem does not cause trouble. Left-eyed cricketers and tennis and golf men probably exist but only in shooting do we hear of it as a dreadful physical problem.

If you learn to shoot without contortions and strain you will be in the same position as the ordinary man who uses his eyes all day without any perceptible strain or discomfort. By adopting a natural head position seventy-five per cent. of the master eye difficulty is solved.

If you are very slightly left-eyed shooting from the right shoulder will not worry you and will in fact train the right eye to function as master.

If you are, on the other hand, completely left-eyed or have lost the sight of the right eye, a particular stock (as illustrated) will compensate for the trouble and allow you to shoot comfortably with the head turned slightly more to the right than is usual.

For the rest, remember that with constant shooting, the right eye gains a natural mastery. It is the eye best placed for supervising aim in the instinctive and unconscious manner which my system directs. In the novice stage of shooting the brain will occasionally be perplexed by receiving left-eye images, but it soon learns to reject them because they show a false aim, the right-eye view being over the centre of the rib, showing the barrels in direct line with the object. With natural eyesight the left-eye image of the gun is in time wholly suppressed, though this eye continues to give valuable aid in seeing the bird and judging its range. There are very few who have not at some stage of their career gone through a course of rifle shooting. In this work the fore-sight, together with a certain amount of barrel, is an object of concentration, and that alone to a great extent fixes the right-eye habit.

XI

SHOOTING DISCOMFORTS AND CURES

Bruised Second Finger.—Caused through loose grip—relaxing grip on firing—badly shaped stock—or bad habit of using pressure of this second finger against the back of the guard to squeeze the trigger pull off. If the stock is gripped too lightly it will occasionally slip through the hands after firing and so knock the finger.

You may wear a finger guard, or unscrew the guard and roll on it an umbrella ring so doubled that will hold in the spur of the guard and take off most of the blow but if you will study the section on Right Hand Grip you will notice that the pulling back of the right hand and the pulling of the trigger with a semi-rigid finger helped by the jar of the gun when it beds home on the shoulder perfectly clears the finger and you will never bruise it if you follow this style of shooting.

Bruised Cheek.—If the face is, say, half an

inch off the stock the recoil is likely to jar
the head into forcible contact. If the head is
too erect and too square the jawbone comes
on to the top of the stock and the jar of recoil
will bruise the flesh. Further, if the head is
too much " down " the cheekbone comes on
to the top of the stock.

Avoid sandwiching your flesh between
either jawbone and stock or cheekbone and
stock, see (section IX) and note that the head
should be pivotted slightly to the right to
prevent jawbone or cheekbone coming into
contact with the stock, and that the gunstock should firmly touch the cheek midway
between the two.

Bruised Mouth is more often than not
caused by the fingers of the right hand
coming back with the recoil : this means
incorrect stance or that the stock is too short
by at least half an inch.

Bruised Arm is due to incorrect stance or
too long a stock.

Bruised Chest is due to incorrect stance
or too short a stock—or insufficient cast
off at toe, or too much toe on stock.

Bruised Shoulder is due to incorrect stance
or too wide a butt.

A recoil pad should cure these ills. Get
one that is rounded at the corners, smooth

and well varnished, and always soft and pneumatic (not hard as the wood itself).

I remember seeing a warning addressed to shooters that they should pay particular attention to the position of the brace buckle. Myself I recommend all who can to dispense with this article while engaged in shooting. A little attention to the fit of the nether garment round the hips and avoidance of a long-waist cut, such as necessitates a high lift of the buttons, will usually render any support other than perhaps a belt unnecessary. The shoulders are more supple without the confining effect of braces and the body less liable to perspiration. But if braces must be worn the buckle should on no account be situated where the butt beds into the shoulder. If the elastic has stretched so as to necessitate this position the remedy is to remove some inches of the webbing and have the fitting re-sewn.

XII

SHAPES OF GUNSTOCK

THE shape of stock which fits one man is not necessarily the best for another man of similar build. A great many factors influence the selection of the best shape of stock for the individual.

The tendency of many modern guns has been toward a grip which is too straight for practical mounting. The line is graceful and it looks well in an illustration but it is a handicap in use (see diagram 1).

The natural stock developed in my new guns is the same in bend and general measurements as the last named, but with very material alterations to the grip. The tang of the action and the trigger plate are curved down so that the weapon mounts naturally parallel to the line of sight without enforcing a strained position of the right arm (see diagram 2).

A third model is a return to a pattern over a century old. This is the keeled or " roach-bellied " shape shown in Diagram 3.

It was copied from an old muzzle-loader and possesses a peculiarly pleasant balance, as well as providing not only a pleasant contour but a comfortable grip.

Trap shooting guns for competition experts need special adaptation to the needs of their specialised shooting position. The " Monte Carlo " (diagram 4) is the basic model. It is also very valuable for game shots with short necks, or for those who find difficulty in mounting an ordinary stock to the face without the butt rising half above the shoulder.

Diagram 5 represents the old flint-lock stock which is occasionally preferred, but represents a return to a gun shape not particularly practical for modern shooting conditions, driven game in particular. The hand or grip is small and comfortable, but is likely to slip through the hand on recoil.

Diagram 6 shows a full left-eyed gunstock, which is occasionally necessary.

Diagrams 7, 8 and 9 represent the development of the pistol-grip in its various degrees of quarter, half, and full. The most appropriate form for the individual depends not only on arm length, width of body and size of hand but also particularly on the type of gun and its special use. This I will proceed to discuss.

Full pistol and half pistol grips are more suitable for single trigger guns than for double triggers, as with the latter there is always a slightly different position of grip with each barrel.   A pistol grip also checks overhead swing.   The full pistol grip therefore is more suitable on the special trap gun or for walking up game and it is seldom seen on the modern game gun.

The half pistol grip is more common.   It is to be preferred to the straight stock in Illustration 1, but the special stock (illustration 2) has all the advantages of the low curved hand of the half pistol grip without any of its disadvantages and would be more likely to suit the majority of sportsmen.

Diagram 10 represents a gun with deepened fore-end.   This hardly concerns stocks, but with certain individuals is a palliative for bad gun mounting.   Except in the case of a man who is disabled or limited in his freedom of physical movement, the need for this amendment suggests that the gun is either badly balanced or does not fit.

XIII

GUN ADJUSTMENTS AND FIELD REPAIRS

THE modern gun as made by a first-class London gunmaker is an arm with an almost indeterminable lease of life. Properly looked after it will endure for year after year without deterioration, but only the very few take the proper amount of care. The duty is usually delegated, and a weapon which costs as much as a piano may receive very superficial treatment. A cleaning rod is inserted into the barrel and the last 15 ins. of barrel is diligently scrubbed—the first 10 or 15 ins. that most need cleaning only feel the brush on its entrance and exit! Fouling collects under the extractors and in the recesses of the action. These and particularly the lumps and flats of the barrels should be wiped clean, also the flats and face of the action. After cleansing, a thorough wipe should be given with an oily rag all over the gun, including trigger blades and barrel ribs. The parts needing oil include the extractor legs, barrel lumps, cocking limbs that project through action, safety slide and fore-end ejector work. Use only a fine lubricating oil very sparingly. For the stock and wood work linseed oil is an excellent dressing, but must on no account be used on the metal work and should be kept clear of the chequering.

It is a wise and economical policy to send in guns for overhaul and thorough cleaning at the end of every season. The owner's cleaning, however thorough, is necessarily limited to externals, but the gunsmith strips the locks and action and makes a general overhaul, besides cleaning and re-lubricating all moving parts. In the process wear and tear are noted and corrected and the gun properly tightened up for the next shooting season. This is more important than is generally realised, for if there is any unduly free play or movement about the action of a gun, and the weapon be fired repeatedly in that state, the hammer action of the firing is likely to exaggerate this small element of wear and tear into a serious looseness.

Bruised, dented or cut barrels are fairly common. A dropped gun, a hasty scramble into a car, or any of the casual bumps of a day's shooting may account for them. There is only one thing to do ; never entrust the gun to the qualified mercies of the local gunsmith,

who may or may not be master of his craft,
but send it back to the maker or to a gunmaker known to be reliable. Barrels are
sensitive things and if any accident occurs
which dents or bruises them at all seriously
DO NOT ATTEMPT TO FIRE CART-
RIDGES THROUGH THE INJURED
TUBE. Rather give up sport for the day
than run risks with an expensive gun.
The primary causes of burst barrels are as
follows : firstly the barrel is indented, secondly
a hard tight-fitting wad meets the obstruction
and turns it into a bulge, finally the smallest
obstruction in the damaged muzzle will burst
the barrel, for the strain flies to the weakest
part and that part is already strained to its
limit.

Repeated use of a dented barrel tends to
wear the internal bulge thin. In extreme
cases it may push it out and so turn the dent
into a bulge. Both render the subsequent
repair more difficult and involve the removal
of important metal in polishing.

There are one or two minor mishaps which
may occur in the field. A loosely fitting
fore-end may drop off the gun while it is
being closed. If the ejector hammers are
down most people find the fore-end impos-
sible to replace. Sometimes it can be put

on when the barrels are in the dropped position. To re-cock the ejector hammers by pressing them hard against a bench or the nearest fence needs some skill. Far easier is to detach the barrels, push out the extractors, attach the fore-end and then press the extractor heads against a fence till they click right home, the click signifying that the ejectors have cocked.

When a single trigger gun jams and the top lever refuses to operate—push the trigger forward and pull the safety catch back.

The cause of a gun jamming is very often to be found in a striker sticking in a cap. The speediest solution of this problem is, if the other barrel is loaded, to fire it in the air, trusting to the jar of recoil to free the errant striker. Then hold the lever open with the thumb and give the gun a sharp jerk. This usually puts matters right and at all events it cannot damage anything except the striker point.

If the lever refuses to open under ordinary pressure hold the gun sideways, put both thumbs one over the other against the lever and the fingers of both hands against the right lock. The amount of pressure from such a squeeze is ever so much more than can be made with one finger and thumb;

after opening look for and remove the cause —it may be either a burst rim or powder residue between barrels and action.

Another embarrassment occurs when a cartridge slips beneath the extractor. This is a case when *force should not be applied*, for there is a danger of " making things worse." First dismount the barrels, pull the extractor out to its limit and if the case cannot be manœuvred into position for extraction it will be necessary to remove the screw holding the extractors, pull them bodily out, remove case and replace them. If the weapon is an ejector, the ejector hammers may need re-cocking in the manner previously explained.

The irregular functioning of ejectors is usually caused either by lack of oil and friction from rust or by the use of wrong kinds of oil which gum the cocking and ejector limbs. If a wash out with petrol and re-lubrication with good gun oil of the limbs protruding from the action fail to remedy the trouble, the gun should be sent for adjustment.

Sometimes a gun action cannot be easily closed. This may be due to an unusually thick-rimmed cartridge, a rare but nevertheless not unavoidable fault in machine-made factory loaded cases, or more often to a slight deposit of fired powder fouling or dirt getting between the barrels and the action, either on the flats of the action, the flats of the barrels, or in the slots of the action. Clean out any accumulation and see that the extractor screw is right home ; if this is loose and projecting it will prevent the gun closing properly.

When assembling, should the barrels refuse to close long before they are in contact with the action the trouble is usually due to a projecting striker catching on the base of the extractor. If the latter is pressed back with the finger the gun will probably close.

The sportsman going abroad is sometimes induced to take cheap or machine-made guns on the assurance that these are quite good enough for the rigours of an expedition where rough usage will be the rule. This is the most fatal of false economies, for in general it can be said the better the gun the worse usage it will withstand. The metal of which cheap and most foreign guns are made is remarkably soft. As a result they shoot and wear loose with astonishing speed. They are not constructed so as to last and though sold at a low price are not cheap in terms of serviceable life. They are seldom worth repairing, for they will give out in a

fresh place almost as soon as the first source
of trouble has been mended. The man
several days away from civilisation of any
kind can, however, effect a temporary repair
if one of these arms " shoots loose " by
simply centre-punching the metal at the
sides of the front lump beneath the barrel
to bring the metal of the hook nearer to the
cross pin or hinge bar and thus close the
breech of the barrels toward the action face,
or if the bolt is loose a light hammering up
of the back lump will enable the bolt to pull
the barrel tighter down to the action.   There
is however neither economy nor reliability in
cheap guns. They may not perhaps be
actively dangerous, but they are invariably
inefficient and unreliable and always pro-
vocative of small delays and embarrassments
in the field.

XIV

INSTRUCTIONS FOR USING AND LOADING A PAIR OF GUNS

A PAIR of guns and a good loader are the equipment of every good shot : undoubtedly the combination is highly effective, and it is doubtful if a good shot would show such a high percentage of kills to cartridges were he to use only a single gun and load it himself.

There are various reasons why you may expect much better performance when using a pair of guns. You are able to keep head and body in " set " position and your eyes on the look-out, whereas with a single gun the disturbance of loading the gun does not help towards such concentration.

Many shooters find their loaders more bother than they are worth, but this is not a fault of the system. Ill-trained loaders make you wait for a gun, they knock barrels, drop guns, hand you an unloaded or partly-loaded gun, etc. On the other hand many good loaders are handicapped through their master not knowing the right thing to do.

I have seen shooters change guns over their left shoulder, over their head and I have heard of a novice with a brand new pair of guns throwing the first gun to the ground to grasp the second gun !

Both shooter and loader must work together to allow smooth and quick exchange of guns.

The shooter must keep his stand and not run about (such fidgety shots disturb adjoining guns).

Even if he has shot on his left and needs the second gun to shoot again on the left he should swing back himself for the gun and not expect the loader to follow him round unless he has a succession of such shots and alters his stand.   He will get his gun quicker, it will be put in the right place in his left hand and there is no chance of " falling on " his loader provided the latter keeps to one position and the shooter always returns to it for exchange of guns.

The shooter after firing either one or both barrels pulls back the safety catch with the right thumb and brings the gun back with the right hand until the muzzle is upright and the breech is near the right of the shoulder. The left hand has meanwhile left the gun as soon as the catch is on " safe " and is thrust

over to the right to receive the loaded gun,
which must be grasped immediately it touches
the hand.

The loader takes the empty gun with his
left hand, and with his right hand simul-
taneously puts the loaded gun into the
shooter's left hand which is extended to
receive it.

The illustrations shows a perfect exchange
of guns, also the diagram shows position of
both the shooter's (A) and the loader's (B)
feet.

It will be seen that the loader is standing
sideways to the shooter and is thus able to
turn his body towards the shooter when
exchanging guns and to turn away from the
shooter to load and close the gun, and to bring
it to the upright.

The loader should have his cartridge bag
slung over his left shoulder with the lid of
the bag folded back and the bag hanging well
in front of the body.

He should take hold of the gun with the
left hand about five or six inches above
the breech and, swinging away from the
shooter, bring the stock under the right arm
on to the right hip, the right hand meanwhile
opening the lever (first finger pressing on
the side of the right lock and thumb on left

side of lever—on no account allowing the
fingers to touch the triggers or even the
guard). With a jerk of the body and a
pull of the left hand he opens the gun and
ejects the fired cases ; whilst doing this his
right hand has left the lever and has gone
to the cartridge bag to get the one or two
cartridges required. (He should never grasp
more than the one or two cartridges required
at the time). His hand is back ready to
insert the cartridges by the time that the
other had completed the opening of the gun.

He should drop the cartridges into the
breech—*not ram them in*. Then with an
upward jerk of the right hip he closes the gun
by *bringing the stock up to the barrels* (never
close a gun by bringing the barrels up to the
stock). The golden rule is that the muzzle
must always be pointing to the ground during
the loading and closing. It should never
point at a spot more than a yard away from
the loader's feet.

Now his right hand grasps the stock, the
gun is lifted upright and the body swung
round ready to push the gun into the shooter's
left hand, at the same instant taking the
fired gun.

In this method of loading both hands are
working at the same time and a remarkable

speed can be attained. I do not recommend the method of holding any cartridges in reserve between the fingers of the right hand. The best of loaders can be seen to fumble with them at times. Your man should be practised or drilled at his work and should start slowly as speed will come with practice.

The shooter should call as he kills his birds—either counting One—Two—Three ; or, Dead—Dead—Miss—Dead. In the latter case the loader counts them up and gives the total at the end of the drive, as the shooter must always know how many birds he has got down. The loader will only mark a fallen bird when told to do so, or when his preoccupations allow.

Remove cartridges after every drive. Carry guns as shown, when they will be quite safe from knocking against each other.

Whenever a gun is carried under the arm it should always be open at the breech. As no loader does this the fact should be noted. Shooters always look kindly on such evidence of safety. Excess of care is never a fault.

XV

HINTS FOR BEGINNERS

IN other pages are some illustrations of the proper way to carry a gun and section XIV will tell you how to load your gun quickly, the only difference being that you get cartridges from your pocket instead of carrying a bag.

Do not fool about with the safety catch—working it to and fro until you do not know whether it is off or on. *Accustom yourself to push it up with the thumb as the gun reaches the " ready " position.*

When walking up always keep in line. When driving never pick up until the drive is over or allow your man to do it.

Never shoot horizontally into hedgerows or covert ; some very remarkable accidents have happened through the shooter not seeing " where his shot was going to end."

For driven birds the shooters are numbered for the first drive : No. 1 being on the left, and thereafter they usually move up two places every drive, thus No. 1 in the first drive will be at No. 3 stand on the second drive, and so on. The reason of moving up two is to save a gun being on the outside twice in succession, so better distributing the chances.

Mark your birds as much as possible and remember how many birds fall in front, on your left, and on your right. Some men are exceptionally good at this, others cannot remember whether "it was five or seven" birds they have got down. Never hang up the field to hunt for a mythical bird.

When walking up game—always go "as steady as a farm labourer." Remember that birds usually prefer to run rather than fly. Partridges if gently pushed forward will run till they are tired or get into cover and will then squat, *but if you walk fast they will run fast and in all probability rise out of range.* If men could remember the number of times they have chased partridges all day without much success and on walking home tired have found birds sit for them, they will realise the importance of slow walking.

See notes on the safe carrying of gun, and always, between drives, carry the gun open when under the arm, it rides better under the arm, and such action is always remembered and appreciated by older shots who *never* fail to notice if a man is a "safe" shot or not.

F

Do not steal other men's birds. *It is your bird when it is coming to you more than to anyone else, or otherwise in your own proper angle of fire.*

Shoot only at an angle of 45° right or left ; do not shoot immediately in front of, or just behind, adjoining guns.

Often two men fire at the same bird. Always let the other man claim it ; it goes into the bag just the same. The lookers-on see most of the game !

The final rule to enable you to do justice to the opportunities coming your way is that put forward in my notes on trap shooting. Forget there are others in the party, perhaps keenly watching your performance, concentrate all your attention on the space which is yours to guard. Take each chance as it arrives to the best advantage, don't allow the mind to dwell on what has gone before nor what may happen later. Live in the moment and disregard all else, except to study the safety and rights of your neighbours. This last becomes a habit and need never be a distraction.

XVI

TRAPSHOOTING

THERE is a great difference between " trapshooting " and pigeon shooting. Trapshooting
or as it was originally called, " clay bird
shooting," is the direct descendant of the old
practice of pigeon shooting. This in its turn
is a direct descendant of the pastime of
" popinjay " shooting, still practised in Fland-
ers and of such antiquity that it is mentioned
in the Iliad and was probably co-eval with the
adoption of the bow as a weapon of war or
chase. The popinjay was a pigeon tethered
by a short length of cord to the top of a tall
mast and capable of restricted flight. With
bows or arbalests a material amount of skill
was needed to hit such a small moving target
with a single projectile.

The development of the art of shooting
flying subsequent to 1760 and the gaming
tendencies of the Waterloo period led to
matches between sportsmen in which live
pigeons thrown by hand from a pit or from
behind a wall furnished the targets.

Towards the middle of the nineteenth century the rules regulating pigeon shooting contests and the guns and loads to be used were more or less codified, and collapsible boxes known as traps were introduced.

During the late Victorian era live pigeon shooting enjoyed a certain social recognition, but during the present century it passed out of keeping with social taste and is now no longer legal in Great Britain, though still practised abroad.

Modern trapshooting employs discs made of a mixture of pitch and pulverised limestone and known as " clay targets," to distinguish them from live birds. Primitive traps or throwers, designed to project either clays or hollow glass balls stuffed with feathers were introduced during the eighties of the last century. These early devices were not very good, and, largely owing to their mechanical imperfections their use did not achieve immediate popularity.

During the last few years very important developments have taken place, and the modern automatic clay target trap has brought about an astonishing change in the sport. Clay bird shooting clubs are increasing rapidly, the number of local clubs being a noteworthy feature.

Independently of their value as one of the pleasantest of summer pastimes and the opportunity they afford for keeping in shooting practice during the close season, they are excellent schools for the novice who wishes to learn how to handle a gun. Clay bird shooting is the most valuable approach to the senior sport. Its educational value is so great that it was adopted during the war as part of the essential training of the fighting branches of the Air Forces of Great Britain, America and France.

Game shots ask " are the conditions of clay bird shooting any use to me as practice for actual game shooting ? " The answer is " they certainly are."

Good shooting depends on a co-ordination of muscular effort, correct stance, correct movements and automatic adherence to certain rules. Trapshooting gives you this practice and a very close approximation to natural conditions. The double rise events particularly afford excellent training, whilst a string of successful shots at clays gives one a " thrill " closely allied to the pleasure of a fine pick-up after a drive. The two are not strictly comparable in all respects, but one may safely say that the " quantity " element in scoring hits on clays is almost as exciting as the " quality " element in game shooting. In addition there is the spur of the competitive element and the pleasure of outdoor recreation in company with those of kindred interests.

Though a shooting man may have ever so much sport of the regular kind he would do well to take part in all trap-shooting meetings that he can conveniently attend. I have often seen really excellent shots seriously perturbed by the presence of a stranger, perhaps a friend of one of the farmers who has come out to see the sport and in all innocence plants himself behind the one member of the party who is easily put off. Public shooting contests are beneficial to all, in that they accustom you to the idea that you can only do your best.   This attitude adopted, the onlookers are soon obliterated from the mind, which is then free to concentrate on the one thing that matters.

XVII

HOW TO SHOOT CLAYS

TRAPSHOOTING differs from game shooting because game rises slowly, gains velocity rapidly and maintains or accelerates speed until out of range. The trap reverses this sequence, the clay being projected at a high velocity which gradually lessens as it reaches the crest of its rise. In practice we remedy this difference by adopting a different technique which meets the conditions inseparable from artificial targets.

THE POSITION IN WHICH THE GUN IS HELD IS DIFFERENT.

This section might just as well be entitled, "How to shoot at moving objects with the gun at the shoulder," as "How to shoot clays," because this position—with the gun ready mounted to the shoulder—is now universally adopted by the best competition shots. It is quicker, and quickness is the imported essence of modern trapshooting.

Stance, grip, and the technique of gun mounting are exactly as previously outlined in the sections on game shooting—but you mount your gun AND POINT IT AT THE TRAP. You do not shoot at the trap, and you do not keep your head down to the stock and remain aiming at the trap. The trap is about to throw a target to a known height, but at an unknown angle of projection. Thus, if your head is down to the stock you will not have adequate freedom of movement for the eye to follow the bird and the gun to follow the eye with accurate alignment in the time.

A close study of the best European and American trapshots reveals the same systematic head movement as the basis of their skill. If their procedure were analysed by a slow motion film we should see that : (1) The gun is mounted to the shoulder and aimed at the trap ; (2) The head is then very slightly eased off the stock ; (3) On the appearance of the target the head moves to it first ; (4) The gun remains pointing at the trap almost until this head movement is completed and is then raised rapidly to the target, which it rapidly overtakes. Discharge occurs on the instant that alignment is obtained.

The whole art of trapshooting is comprised

in the ability to take instantaneous aim and pull the trigger practically without visible swing. Speed is all essential. The quick shot has a very marked advantage over the slow shot where clays are concerned, for his speed gives him what is for the moment an apparently stationary target.

If we examine the flight of a clay target we find that it is thrown by the trap to a distance of forty-five to fifty-five yards. At about fifteen or twenty yards from the trap it reaches the zenith of its curve. For the next ten yards or so it travels a practically horizontal course. Viewed from the gun stand it appears to be hovering, although in point of fact it is still moving rapidly away from the shooter. This is the position in which the quick shot takes the target. At the end of its horizontal flight it loses momentum and begins to fall earthward with a pronounced dip. The slower shot who only comes into action at this stage has thus a more difficult target to tackle than that of his swifter competitor, independent of the fact that targets which have lost their spin are harder to break, also at the increased range a target may pass unbroken through the gaps in a pattern, by now become wide.

The quick shot has the choice of any

relative point during the transit of the target over the flatter portion of its curve of flight. An expert selects the precise point where he knows his gun will give its best killing pattern.

Items to be remembered.—Everything included in the instructions with regard to stance, grip and gun handling.

DON'T put your left hand too far up the barrel, because this makes you shoot behind your right hand targets.

The eye must never be brought down to the rib—the rib should be brought up to the eye.

When mounting a gun at the trap, bed the butt in the right part of the shoulder and do not shift it again.

See that the trigger pull of your gun is both quick and sweet. It must respond instantly. A bad trigger pull is fatal to good trapshooting.

POINT THE LEFT HAND AT THE BIRD.

A.

B.

C.

A. Everyone knows that with every kill the gunmuzzle must have been pointed correctly.

B. Shooters often do not fully realize the fact that as the barrels lie in the left hand this also must have been pointed in the right place.

C. THE LEFT HAND MUST NOT BE CONSIDERED SIMPLY AS A LIFTING LEVER. YOU WILL SHOOT JUST WHEREVER YOU PUT IT AND THEREFORE IT MUST POINT THE GUN AT THE BIRD DURING THE WHOLE PERIOD OF GUNMOUNTING AND NOT MISUSE IT TO FIRSTLY LIFT THE GUN AND FINALLY POKE IT AT THE OBJECT.

See page 36

SHAPES OF GUNSTOCK.

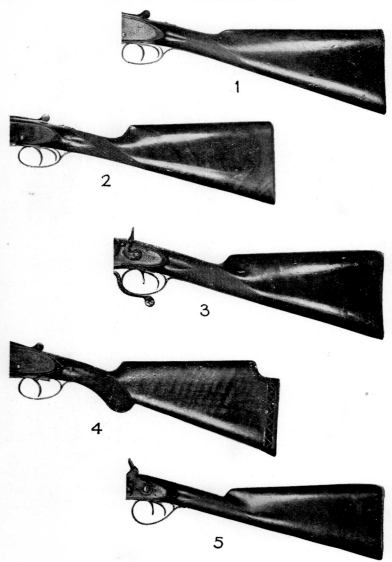

See page 62

SHAPES OF GUNSTOCK.

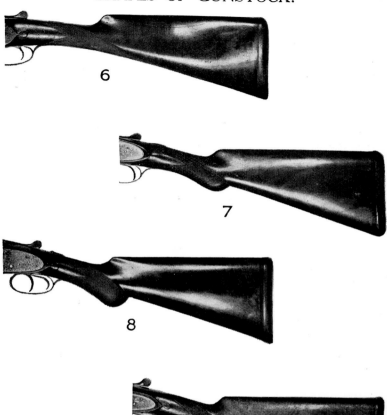

LOADING AND USING A PAIR OF GUNS.

The loader has turned with muzzles erect and now with his back to the shooter is bringing down the gun.

Ejecting the fired cases and reloading.

Gun muzzles erect and turning towards the shooter.

The shooter brings back the fired gun with his right hand and extends the left across it for the fresh gun. Throughout the loader has not altered his stance.

See page 72

XVIII

TESTING STOCK FIT

THE man who is away from civilisation
may feel doubtful about the fit of his gun
and wish to test it. To do this he should
cut a finely, pointed piece of paper and shut it
in the breech absolutely central with the rib,
so that the point stands up one-eighth of an
inch above the barrels. This point is the
back sight. Next with equal care fasten
a precisely similar point at the muzzle end to
serve as a foresight.

Then with both eyes open and holding the
gun in the " ready " position look at an object
and mount the gun at it.

Close the eyes a fraction of a second *before*
the gun is drawn right home to the shoulder
—*then before* you pull the trigger open the
eyes and observe where your sights are really
pointing.

Practice this at various objects or points
of aim, and you may find that though you
may be " dead on " for straight-away shots,
and, say, shots to your left, you are aiming

over or behind in the case of shots to your right or overhead.

In order to avoid a false stance move the feet after each shot, and above all avoid adjusting yourself to an artificial and temporary fit to the gun, the idea being to take these snapshots as naturally as possible. The information to be gained from this experiment is limited to the discovery that your failure at certain shots is in all probability due rather to the poor fit of your gun than to any other cause.

For a more critical analysis an outdoor shooting test can be made without the paper sights. If a whitewashed steel or iron target, about three foot square, is available this is best, but if it is not you can extemporise an adequate test butt by sticking double sheets of newspaper on a wood frame or on a hedge. See that the print is right way up so that you will know afterwards which is the top or bottom of the pattern.

In the centre of the target mark a big ink aiming spot, then measure off—do not pace it, but measure it exactly—a firing point at sixteen yards.

Assuming the eye is thirty-six inches from the gun muzzle, also that the gun shoots with true elevation and the two barrels in the same line, then errors in bend and cast-off will be magnified sixteen times on the target.

Fire several snap shots at the target with your normal stance, then take the centre of your composite pattern as the average. If your charge is centred two inches *below* the point of aim, the stock certainly needs straightening one-eighth of an inch. A group two inches high represents a nicely placed pattern. If higher, for every two inches surplus elevation the stock should be bent down one-eighth of an inch. A group one inch to the left would involve an increase of cast-off of one-sixteenth of an inch, while three inches to the right would involve a reduction of cast-off by three-sixteenths of an inch.

There is always a possibility that the shooter rather than the gun is at fault, hence, any consistent error should be further tested, not only in terms of the gun but in terms of gun mounting as well. The following rules apply :—

POSITION OF THE SHOTS ON THE TARGET AND EXPLANATION.

Shooting on the Right.—Causes may be : (*a*) too much cast-off ; (*b*) head too far forward with eye too far over the stock; (*c*) stock too short; (*d*) incorrect stance.

Shooting on the Left.—Causes may be: (*a*) not enough cast-off; (*b*) stock too long; (*c*) pulling in with left hand; (*d*) stock on the arm instead of into the shoulder.

Shooting Low.—Causes may be: (*a*) too much bend of stock; (*b*) too heavy a pull; (*c*) flinching; (*d*) left hand not far enough forward or a badly balanced gun that is heavy forward and shoots low.

Shooting High.—Causes may be: (*a*) stock too straight at the bump; (*b*) too light a pull; (*c*) too long a stock; (*d*) too much " toe " to stock.

If the stock is finally proved to be at fault it should be altered by an expert who has seen you shoot.   Self-gunfitting is very much like self-doctoring—not by any means a certain cure! Nevertheless, to suspect a malady is the first step in locating it and putting yourself in the way of a cure.

XIX

COMPETITION PSYCHOLOGY

In clay target shooting just as in any other competitive sport, or as in war, morale counts for a very great deal. Variations in temperament are so wide that no one system of advice will apply to all individuals. The naturally phlegmatic shot does not perhaps need advice, but the quickest shots are usually rather highly strung individuals whose swiftness of thought and action is the reflex of abnormally swift response to external happenings.

They are quicker to receive impressions, also more likely to be bothered about them.

Every captain of a team knows the difficulty of the man whose individual performance is excellent yet who is likely to go to pieces with nervous excitement when in the stress of a competition where he owes duty to others.

There is only one way to eliminate this disturbing element. It is so simple, so self-evident as to be rarely mentioned, yet if mentioned the advice works wonders.

The secret is absolute concentration, not on the competition, nor on the series of shots, not even on the score or any other broad aspect of the occasion, but on each successive shot without reference to its predecessors or those to come.

Concentrate on each shot as an entirely independent all-important thing in itself. Forget and designedly shut out everything else.

There is no spare time in trapshooting competitions. Quite immaterial to you at the moment is what your competitors are doing. The less you know about them the better.

A good shot on the firing line concentrates on preparing HIMSELF. He finds that after taking each shot he has just sufficient time, without haste or effort, to eject the fired cartridge, take a fresh one, examine it to see if it is correct, reload, come to the " ready " position and recover correct stance and balance—then it is his turn to fire again !

Never allow yourself to become over-confident—this breeds carelessness. Concentrate on every shot. Make each shot the start of the competition so far as you are concerned.

Ignore YOUR SCORE and, of course, that of others.

Target by target, that is the only thing to interest you.

Forget there is a finish. The score book always shows up the man who counts his score, he usually starts well and finishes badly.

There is only one competitor to beat—that is the bird.

You have not to beat others, their success or failure is their own business, not yours.

The finest shot on earth cannot do more than kill his bird, and if you keep on killing there is no one on earth who can beat you.

If you treat your last best scores as your true competitor you will get the right spirit of competition, which is to be a good winner and an extra good loser.

In an earlier chapter I recommended competitive trap shooting as a fine education for the game shot, and I appeal to the finished performers in the field or at the covert-side to confirm me when I say that the attitude here described is the ideal one for game as well. In trap shooting it is essential, in game shooting invaluable—trap shooting teaches you to adopt the policy of concentration better than anything else.

G

XX

GAME GUNS OF TO-DAY

THERE has been very little progressive
development in sporting guns since the
modern conventional side lock double ejector
became more or less standardised in the last
decade of the nineteenth century. There has
been a certain amount of detail improvement,
such as steel barrels replacing Damascus,
but to all intents many makers are still
regularly turning out a gun with little if any
variation from their model of a quarter
century ago.

A survey of my own firm's practice shows
that most modifications of design have been
in the nature of a simplification of lock and
ejector mechanisms. New steels have been
selected and particular attention has been
paid, not so much to *reduction of weight* as
to its *better distribution* in barrels and action.
Coincidently, there has been an all-round
increase in hidden strength to meet conditions
liable to be imposed by modern powders.
These matters are important but they do not

strike the eye, their effect on external appearance is practically nil.

Broadly speaking, the modern gun may be pronounced 20 per cent. better balanced, 30 per cent. stronger, and 40 per cent. less likely to fail in functioning details.

A certain amount of attention has been paid to the under-and-over gun, really a "throw-back" to the oldest type of double barrel construction. These guns enjoy a sporadic vogue as novelties, but it is certain that they present no great feature of convenience or utility such as may enable them to supplant the side-by-side gun. On the other hand they suffer from very definite mechanical handicaps which cannot be ignored. They should be regarded rather as a fad or novelty than as a seriously competing type.

The single trigger action represents a detail improvement of considerable utility, detachable locks on the other hand are at best a refinement of dubious value, but neither variation, nor the under-and-over type of gun, represents definite radical progress comparable with the noteworthy developments of the past.

In the last twenty-five years a certain improvement has been registered in barrel boring. Constant experiment has enabled us to evolve methods which give a very improved pattern at 40 yards. What was unusual in the old days has become habit since. For instance, it was exceptional to find a gun which would consistently give 70 per cent. patterns at forty yards. To-day we are able to get this standard 70 per cent. of pellets in the 30 in. circle at 40 yards with absolute certainty. Very often we exceed this average by an additional 5 or 10 per cent. Corresponding improvement has been effected in the lesser degrees of choke, with proportionate gain of efficiency for all departments of service.

The sportsman is not interested in detailed technicalities relating to the boring of barrels, but he is interested in the practical application of these improved results on game. Some recent experimental research of mine, now applied to all guns I turn out, showed that a new form of boring, giving the normal standard patterns up to 40 yards, exhibited a marked improvement at ranges beyond forty yards. In other words the charge of shot maintains a better formation at long range. The inference is that the old-fashioned or standard type of choke and cone unduly disturbed the pellets, so that the charge had lost cohesion before reaching the forty yards target. My theory or conjecture is that the pellets in the top half of the shot cartridge—if it were sectioned parallel to the long axis of the barrels—would be found at the bottom half of the target, while those in the lower half would be concentrated in the top section of the target. As distance increases the diversion of pellets due to this unrealised crossing effect would emphasise separation, so that the patterns at fifty and sixty yards were so wide that no killing effect could be relied on.

With my new type of boring I do find that though the patterns shown by the guns are normal at forty yards they retain effectiveness for a material distance beyond. How bad ordinary patterns are may be inferred from the fact that it is almost an even money chance that if you shoot at your hat at sixty yards not a pellet will touch it.

This interesting progress in boring is associated with the extremely important modern development of the short barrelled gun.

Modern conditions and requirements call for maximum strength and shooting qualities, minimum weight compatible with low recoil, perfect balance and something beyond the poise and ease of manipulation characteristic of the best examples of ordinary guns. The

25 in. barrelled gun may be taken as marking in these respects a noteworthy change between the late nineteenth century guns and those needed to-day.

The old 30 in. barrel is a relic of past ages and is purely a survival from the black powder period. It has long been common knowledge that smokeless powder would permit a very radical reduction of barrel length, but conservative tendencies amounting to prejudice suggested that this reduction could only be made at the expense of pattern and penetration.

In the first edition of this book I said :

" In point of fact almost all velocity is generated with smokeless powders within a few inches of the chamber, and is not materially increased as the charge approaches the muzzle. The shooting or pattern is however regulated at the muzzle end of the barrel independent of length. It does not matter whether the muzzle is 30 or 25 in. from the breech ; the velocity of the charge is not affected and the pattern has to be regulated by the usual methods of control.

" A century ago a barrel of less than 36 in. long would have been derided. With the establishment of the early breech-loaders, firing the same charge of powder and the

same kind of powder as the old muzzle
loaders, barrels shortened to 30 in. At the
close of the century the demand for light guns
for driven game reduced the length to 28 in.
To-day the modern 25 in. is not only as good
as the longer barrels of the obsolescent type
in that it shoots as strongly and gives as
good a pattern, but it is, paradoxically,
perhaps, even better at longer ranges than
the old-length barrels. In addition to this
superiority in the all-important matter of
performance it has further advantages of its
own.

"The short barrelled 25 in. gun shows an
improvement in weight, in balance and in
ease of handling. The reduction of the
effort needed in gun mounting allows steadier
yet quicker shooting."

This passage gave offence to the *Field*
reviewer, who stated in the issue of October
22, 1925 :

"The statement that the velocity of the
charge is not affected by reducing the barrels
from 30 inches to 25 inches is absurd. As
a matter of fact the shorter barrels actually
develop about 100 f.s. less muzzle velocity
than the longer ones with standard cartridges.
We agree that for practical purposes of sport
this reduction will have little, if any, effect,

but we cannot pass the statement that a reduction of 5 inches in barrel length has no effect on the muzzle velocity."

This led to correspondence, and after two letters the paper refused further space for discussion and cut short the correspondence.

Now shot gun velocities are never taken as muzzle velocities, but over 20 yards, starting, of course, from the muzzle. Over that distance the commonly occurring difference between 25 and 30-inch barrels is usually well under 40 feet per second and the *Field*, although repeatedly challenged by me, has never put forward a particle of proof to justify its astonishing statement that the difference grows to 100 at the muzzle. Muzzle velocity cannot be measured, it can only be inferred, but while this inference is exact in the case of rifle bullets the changing form of a shot charge forbids calculation. Recoil measurements in presence of different grades of velocity offer an important clue and these prove the *Field* value a pernicious exaggeration.

The introduction of a purely theoretical figure of loss estimated as 100 f.s. *at the muzzle* is likely to be misleading to sportsmen who are accustomed to reading of loads and cartridges which give a certain mean velocity.

This is always taken over 20 yards, and confusion is bound to result if we are suddenly switched off from tangible fact to vague and unsupported hypothesis.

During the succeeding year I experimented widely with many varieties of loads and different powders. The results do not bear out the contention of the *Field* reviewer, but many curious facts have emerged. As the *Field* in the above quotation admits: a difference of 100 f.s. muzzle velocity " would have little if any effect so far as practical purposes of sport are concerned." I say that if it did exist it would matter a great deal; as it doesn't why bother.

A very wide range of tests at 20 yards show that a figure of 43 f.s. average holds good at that range. In some cases the 25 in. showed a higher velocity than the longer 30 in. barrels, in others the difference was negligible, but an average taken over a wide range of different loads shows that the average variation is 43 f.s. This amount is negligible, particularly when we consider that variations in excess of this occur in almost every half-dozen of the very best loaded cartridges; also, the variation at 20 yards between the 25 in. barrel and the usual modern game gun of 28 in. is even less.

Let us accept this 40 f.s. loss at 20 yards as a concession to theorists, for, needless to say, it has no practical effect on killing game at ordinary ranges, and let us consider what advantages the shooter reaps from the reduction of barrel length and removal of misplaced weight of metal.

It has been suggested that the short barrels were more difficult to align and that the eye missed the guidance afforded by the extra length of barrels. This argument would, even if it were true, only hold good in the case of those very rare shots who actually aim their guns almost as a rifle is aimed. In their case they are not so much influenced by barrel length as by " apparent barrel length " and they are the victims of an optical illusion.

A well-known authority on fire-arms, Major H. B. C. Pollard, writing in *Country Life*, March 14, 1925, in an article on " Why the short barrelled gun is best," says :

" A more effective ground for criticism of the short barrel is that the eye, accustomed to guidance along the top rib to the foresight, so to speak, misses the customary extra 5 in. of barrel, and that the short gun at first gives ' a sense of something missing.' This is very plausible, but I am not altogether certain whether it really means anything.

" The game shot is seldom conscious of his foresight at all. His eye is on the bird, and it is only *after discharge* that the muzzles lift momentarily and give him a glimpse of half a foot of barrel. He certainly 'sees' the barrels as they come up to the line of sight, but he should not have them in focus.

" I am inclined to believe that the ' sense of something missing ' is purely psychological and entirely illusory. Whether it is a visual illusion is open to doubt, for, if a large foresight improvised out of a bead of sealing-wax is applied to a standard game gun of 28 in. or 30 in. barrel, the barrel appears shortened, and a 25 in. barrel with a small foresight appears comparatively longer than the other.

" It follows that, if the ' sense of something missing ' is due to an optical illusion, a small foresight on the short gun compensates for it. If, on the other hand, it is, as I suspect, psychological rather than actual, and due to the unanticipated swiftness of response of the short gun, it will vanish as soon as the new gun is used in the field or at practice at clays, and is a testimony to the handiness of the new type. After all, driving a different kind of car for the first time often produces a feeling of strangeness, but it has never been suggested that progress in car development should be restricted because of this transient feeling of difference."

This clear elucidation not only explains the point at issue but will interest many of the earlier users of short barrelled guns. These as originally built had the usual wide shot gun rib with the ordinary foresight, and in consequence gave a noticeable impression of shortness until the eye became accustomed to them.

To-day the later short barrelled guns are made with a special form of rib and sights in strict proportion. The rib taper is specially designed to harmonise with the perspective effect of the barrels as seen by the eye when the gun is mounted to the shoulder. The result is astonishingly effective, for a 25 in. barrel gun is thus made to convey to the eye the effect of a full 30 inches. It can even be made to appear longer.

It is now some years since the 25 in. gun was first brought out, and I think we may take it that shooting men are conservative, and rightly so. A man does not willingly abandon the gun with which he knows he can shoot, besides, no magic of salesmanship can deceive him as to its performances in the field. If the short barrelled 25 in. gun had been bad, we should have heard about it long ago. Enraged and disappointed people would have cried aloud for vengeance. This has not happened, the pioneer type of sportsman tried the new 25 in. gun, he verified the merits claimed on its behalf, and he has stuck to it for the one simple reason that it was entirely efficient and in several respects an advance on the conventional specification.

To-day many first-class London makers of best guns advertise 25 in. guns, but it may be some little time before they pick up the nice points of construction which, with the lead of twenty years of experience, I as the pioneer designer of the type have gradually evolved.

The demand for a 25 in. barrelled gun among the sporting public rests on a perfectly sound basis. They have seen the more alert and intelligent among their companions using 25 in. guns—Churchill's, as a rule—carrying less weight, shooting better than usual, and —satisfied. If you see an older man in the next butt wiping your eye and observe that his barrels are 25—well !

There has been opposition. No one can suggest that my efforts received immediate recognition at the hands of the sporting press nor that my colleagues of the gun industry welcomed and supported the new departure. In these circumstances I owe more than casual gratitude to those individual pioneers who turned up brazenly with these unconventional short barrels among the critical and conservative long-barrelled majority, and had the courage to say, " This is a new and a better thing." They proved it.

To-day the strangeness has shifted the other way round. The young man, youthfully sensitive to the opinion of others, would no more appear with 30 in. barrels without excuse or deprecation than he would bear his great-grandfather's muzzle-loaders to the moor. His grandfather, still alert and active, is philosopher enough to know that his cast-offs will suffice for the boy, but that he, consulting his own pleasure and comfort, can add a decade to his sporting life by relegating cumbersome old guns to a younger generation and using a pair of perfectly balanced short barrelled 25's. The beginner should, if possible, never start behind the times ; rather should he aim at being an exponent of his own time.

My experience—and this is an opinion which should count for a good deal—is briefly as follows :

Many years devoted to giving instruction

in shooting have clearly shown that it takes approximately four times as much ammunition and four times as many hours of practice to enable the average individual to attain a moderate standard of efficiency with the long barrel as to reach the same stage with the 25 in. short barrel.

Years were necessary to learn the really perfect handling of the old long guns. To-day the short gun, with its far, far better balance, becomes " part of yourself " in a quarter or less of the time. The first season or so with the old guns was always a matter of " chance it." With the new type " sense of direction " is quickly achieved ; success is not the pursuit of a fugitive dream, but a goal by no means difficult of attainment. The appeal of the 25 in. gun is not to the imagination, it does not depend on chance successes or anything except its own virtues. It is easier to shoot with—best of all to shoot really well with—and not less effective in pattern and penetration than any of the old long barrelled types. Essentially modern in its adaptation to the modern cartridge it dismisses the obsolete past. It has been re-designed in every detail, re-balanced, fined down and perfected during twenty years of careful critical and invariably progressive work. It

is harmonious within itself and in tune with
its partner, the modern cartridge.

The gunmaker who knows no better than
to supply his customer with the old standard
fowling piece, having barrels shortened to
25 in., is bound to meet with disappointment.
I have scrapped more than one convention
in manufacture and re-designed throughout.
My "xxv" gun is not a wedding of old with
new, it has been re-born. I claim for it that
it handles like a 20 bore, shoots as hard as a
10 bore, looks as long as a 30 in. when aligned
on a bird, it seems to quicken the faculties
and is always twice as comfortable to carry.

The new short gun has proved fully
adequate under the severe test of wild-
fowling and, by inference, any shooting
abroad which necessitates taking shots beyond
the range considered orthodox on preserved
ground, whether the game is walked-up or
driven. The Heath "Chamberless" system
of boring has been specialised to meet the
wildfowler's needs at home ; but it involves
the use of thin-brass cases (formerly known
as " Perfects ") which are not readily obtainable and can only be loaded by those having
the necessary experience. Though the case
is 12 bore its interior is 10 bore, hence the
long chamber takes any length of case—

chamber and barrel being the same bore, or nearly so. A number of successful XXV guns have been built on this principle.

For the sportsman abroad, dependent on local supplies of ammunition, much more interesting is the XXV specially built for $2\frac{3}{4}$ or 3-inch paper cases, which are everywhere obtainable. Short barrels are ideal for meeting the conditions presented. Such guns must be made rather heavy, but by dispensing with the unnecessary inches of muzzle and keeping the weight amidships a really handy gun can be produced, a revelation to those who associate heavily loaded cartridges with a cumbersome and awkward gun to fire them. Rubber butt, snugly fitting stock and sturdy barrels free of nerve racking vibration reduce the *sensation* of recoil to something closely approaching normal. As to pattern and penetration the rule holds good that short barrels satisfy every practical test and give in addition what may be summarised as superior charge delivery.

The tradition of having ultra long barrels for heavy charge guns dates back to black powder days when the propellent was made in a variety of grain sizes, the larger needing a long barrel in which to evolve their power.

H

The finer grain powders gave too much pressure when exploded behind heavy charges of shot. Smokeless powders are subject to the same principles, but the adjustment is more conveniently effected, namely, by holding up the reserve gases till the shot has moved an extra inch or two out of the chamber, when the risk of unduly elevating the pressure has passed. Hence, as with game charges, the important rise of the velocity curve is concentrated in the rear end of the barrel.

The mention of wild-fowl guns on the XXV system almost compels reference to small bores. Up to date the gain in handiness of the standard calibre has met the need of those who contemplate a sixteen or twenty. But, granting that the benefits conferred will be proportional, time alone is needed to exploit the possibilities of the XXV in the lesser calibres, even to the 28 bore and the ·410. We know their killing power already, but they are seldom seen in the modern form.